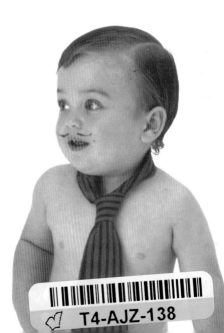

It's a Boy!

Ariel Books

**Andrews McMeel
Publishing**

Kansas City

It's a Boy!

A Book of Quotations

EDITED BY Mary Rodarte

PHOTOGRAPHS BY Julie Gang

Photographs copyright © 1999 by Julie Gang

www.andrewsmcmeel.com

ISBN: 0-7407-0070-7
Library of Congress Catalog
Card Number: 99-60621

Contents

Introduction

Congratulations on your new baby boy! After what may have seemed like an eternity of waiting, he has finally made his grand entrance. As you hold your new son, marvel at his tender skin, his new baby smell, and the downy hair on his head. What a beautiful creation you've brought into the world!

There's a new member in your family, and you've got a lot of time to get to know each other. Who is this little boy and who will he become? What's going on behind those wise baby eyes? What is it that makes him laugh or cry?

Hard work, endless diaper

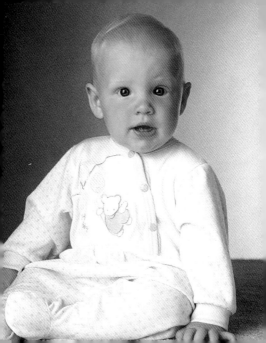

I T ' S *A* *B O Y !*

changing, and many sleepless nights lie ahead. But when you look at that little person, given to you to protect, to guide, to love, you know it's all worth it—he's priceless. As you read this book, celebrate the mishaps, the mischief, and the miracle of your precious baby boy.

Welcome,

Baby Boy!

I
T
'
S

A

B
O
Y
!

After the baby was born, I remember thinking that no one had ever told me how much I would love my child.

—Nora Ephron

What a difference it makes to come home to a child!

—Margaret Fuller

As often as I have wit-
nessed the miracle, held
the perfect creature with
its tiny hands and feet,
each time I have felt as
though I were entering a
cathedral with prayer in
my heart.

—Margaret Sanger

When I approach a child, he inspires in me two sentiments: tenderness for what he is, and respect for what he may become.

—Louis Pasteur

I do not love him because he is good but because he is my child.

—Rabindranath Tagore

*I
T
'
S

A

B
O
Y

!*

There is no other closeness in human life like the closeness between a mother and her baby: Chronologically, physically, and spiritually, they are just a few heartbeats away from being the same person.

—Susan Cheever

Don't be afraid to kiss
your baby when you feel
like it.
—Dr. Benjamin Spock

Every baby born into the
world is a finer one than
the last.
—Charles Dickens

And now [my child] makes every day like Christmas. I can't wait to see him in the morn-ing. I can't wait for him to wake up.

—Kirstie Alley

I
T
'
S

A

B
O
Y
!

The baby was a lovely little boy, but sad to say, he did not weigh sixty pounds. That is what I had gained and that was what I had to lose.

—Barbara Bush

I think of my children's births—carry them around with me every day of my life.

—Joyce Maynard

The first handshake in life is the greatest of all: the clasp of an infant's fist around a parent's finger.

—Mark Beltaire

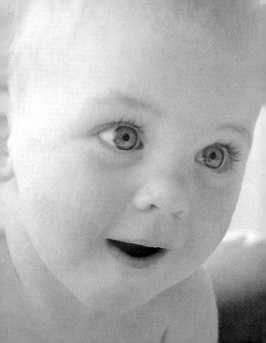

Romance fails us and so
do friendships, but the
relationship of parent and
child, less noisy than all
the others, remains indel-
ible and indestructible, the
strongest relationship on
earth.

—Theodore Reik

I T ' S   A   B O Y !

I begin to love this little creature, and to anticipate his birth as a fresh twist to a knot, which I do not wish to untie.
— Mary Wollstonecraft Shelley

Making the decision to have a child—it's momentous. It is to decide forever to have your heart go walking around outside your body.
— Elizabeth Stone

I remember leaving the hospital . . . thinking, "Wait, are they going to let me just walk off with him? I don't know beans about babies! I don't have a license to do this. [We're] just amateurs."

—Anne Tyler

While you can quarrel with a grown-up, how can you quarrel with a newborn baby who has stretched out his little arms for you to pick him up?

—Maria von Trapp

Sleep,

Baby, Sleep

The art of being a parent is to sleep when the baby isn't looking.

—Anonymous

Families with babies and families without babies are sorry for each other.
—Edgar Watson Howe

I actually remember feeling delight, at two o'clock in the morning, when the baby woke for his feed, because I so longed to have another look at him.
—Margaret Drabble

For the first six months or so, your opponent has been unable to escape. Alas, the rules are about to change drastically. . . . The enemy is now mobile.

—Peter Mayle

People who say they sleep like a baby usually don't have one.

—Leo J. Burke

I love the child just
falling asleep;
Give him a golden dream
to keep!

—Marceline
Desbordes-Valmore

I T'S A B O Y !

Home alone with a wakeful newborn, I could shower so quickly that the mirror didn't fog, and the backs of my knees stayed dry.

— Marni Jackson

If men had to have babies they would only ever have one each.

— Diana, Princess of Wales

There never was a child so lovely but his mother was glad to get him asleep.
—Ralph Waldo Emerson

"You agreed to get up nights."

This is true. I stumble into the nursery, pick up my son, so small, so perfect, and as he fastens himself to me like a tiny, sucking minnow I am flooded with tenderness.
—Sara Davidson

The most amazing moment was when he was handed to me in his little blan-ket and looked at me with his huge blue eyes.

—Margaret Drabble

I
T
,
S

A

B
O
Y

!

In point of fact, we are all born rude. No infant has ever appeared yet with the grace to understand how inconsiderate it is to disturb others in the middle of the night.

—Judith Martin
("Miss Manners")

Mothers

and Sons

I T ' S A B O Y !

There aren't words yet invented to define the emotions a mother feels as she cuddles her newborn child.

—Janet Leigh

I had a baby. He was beautiful and mine. Totally mine. No one had bought him for me.

—Maya Angelou

I am persuaded that there is no affection of the human heart more exquisitely pure, than that which is felt by a grateful son towards a mother.

—Hannah More

Men are what their mothers made them.

—Ralph Waldo Emerson

I love his laugh. It bubbles out in an infectious, whole-hearted way. This is pure joy—nothing else matters.
—Anne Morrow Lindbergh

The god to whom little boys say their prayers has a face very much like their mother's.
—J. M. Barrie

I
T
'
S

A

B
O
Y
!

There is one picture so beautiful that no painter has ever been able to perfectly reproduce it, and that is the picture of the mother holding in her arms her babe.
—William Jennings Bryan

A son and his mother are godly.
—Rochelle Owens

Sons are the anchors of a mother's life.

—Sophocles

A mother's love for her child is like nothing else in the world. It knows no law, no pity, it dares all things and crushes down remorselessly all that stands in its path.

—Agatha Christie

Begin, baby boy, to recognize your mother with a smile. —Virgil

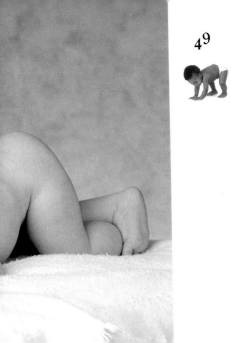

I
T
'
S

A

B
O
Y
!

My mama raised me right.
—Elvis Presley

A babe at the breast is as much pleasure as the bearing is pain.
—Marion Zimmer Bradley

It's such a powerful con-
nection; it takes me by
surprise. I feel like there's a
dotted line connecting me
to my son.

—Sarah Langston

IT'S A BOY!

The tie is stronger than that between father and son and father and daughter. . . . The bond is also more complex than the one between mother and daughter. For a woman, a son offers the best chance to know the mysterious male existence.

—Carole Klein

He's His

Father's Son

I
T
'
S

A

B
O
Y
!

If you can give your son only one gift, let it be enthusiasm.

—Bruce Barton

It is not flesh and blood but the heart that makes us fathers and sons.

—Friedrich von Schiller

It never occurs to a boy that someday he will be as dumb as his father.
—Mark Twain

The sooner you treat your son as a man, the sooner he will be one.
—John Dryden

You are worried about seeing him spend his early years in doing nothing. What! Is it nothing to be happy? Nothing to skip, play, and run around all day long? Never in his life will he be so busy again.

—Jean-Jacques Rousseau

I
T
'S

A

B
O
Y
!

Before I got married I had
six theories about bringing
up children; now I have six
children and no theories.
—John Wilmot,
Earl of Rochester

Of all nature's gifts to the
human race, what is sweeter
to a man than his children?
—Cicero

What are little boys
   made of?
Snips and snails, and
   puppy dogs' tails;
That's what little boys are
   made of.

      —Anonymous

Sons have a rebellious
wish to be disillusioned by
that which charmed their
fathers.

      —Aldous Huxley

Yours is the Earth and
everything that's in it,
And—which is more—
you'll be a Man, my
son!

—Rudyard Kipling

*I
T
,
S

A

B
O
Y
!*

He that will have his son
have a respect for him and
his orders, must himself have
a great reverence for his son.

—John Locke

Nearly every man is a firm
believer in heredity until his
son makes a fool of himself.

—Herbert V. Prochnow

'Tis a happy thing
To be the father unto
   many sons.
   —William Shakespeare

Every father knows at once
too much and too little
about his own son.
                    —Fanny Fern

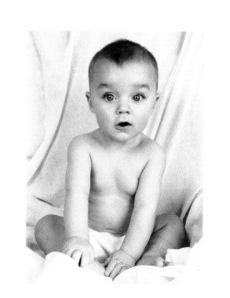

Wat was silent in the father speaks in the son; and often I've found the son the unveiled secret of the father.

—Friedrich Nietzsche

I
T
'
S

A

B
O
Y
!

My lovely living boy,
My hope, my hap, my love,
my life, my joy.
—Guillaume de Salluste,
Seigneur du Bartas

Bringing up

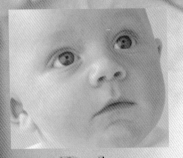

Baby

I
T
'
S

A

B

O

Y

!

One of the most important things to remember about infant care is: Never change diapers in midstream.

—Don Marquis

If you want a baby, have a new one. Don't baby the old one.

—Jessamyn West

All babies look like me.
— Winston Churchill

There is nothing more thrilling in this world, I think, than having a child that is yours, and yet is mysteriously a stranger.
— Agatha Christie

Keeping a baby requires a good deal of time, effort, thought, and equipment, so unless you are prepared for this, we recommend that you start with a hamster, whose wants are far simpler.

—Elinor Goulding Smith

I
T
'
S

A

B
O
Y
!

A child can never be better
than what his parents think
of him.

—Marcelene Cox

Train up a child in the way
he should go,
and when he is old he will
not depart from it.

—Proverbs 22:6

If a child is to keep alive his inborn sense of wonder he needs the companionship of at least one adult who can share it, rediscovering with him the joy, excitement, and mystery of the world we live in.

—Rachel Carson

Does it seem impossible that the child will grow up? That the bashful smile will become a bold expression . . . that a briefcase will replace the blue security blanket?

—Anne Beattie

I
T
'S

A

B
O
Y
!

If a child lives with approval,
he learns to like himself.
—Dorothy Law Nolte

Too much indulgence has
ruined thousands of chil-
dren; too much *Love* not one.
—Fanny Fern

Loving a child doesn't mean giving in to all his whims; to love him is to bring out the best in him, to teach him to love what is difficult.

—Nadia Boulanger

Before I had children I always wondered whether their births would be, for me, like the ultimate in my gym class failures. And discovered, instead . . . that I'd finally found my sport.

— Joyce Maynard

This book was composed in Bembo
with display in Pabst.

Book design and composition by
JUDITH STAGNITTO ABBATE
of Abbate Design
Doylestown, Pennsylvania